CRITTERS' CRAZY CLUES

WHY DO BATS SLEEP UPSIDE DOWN?

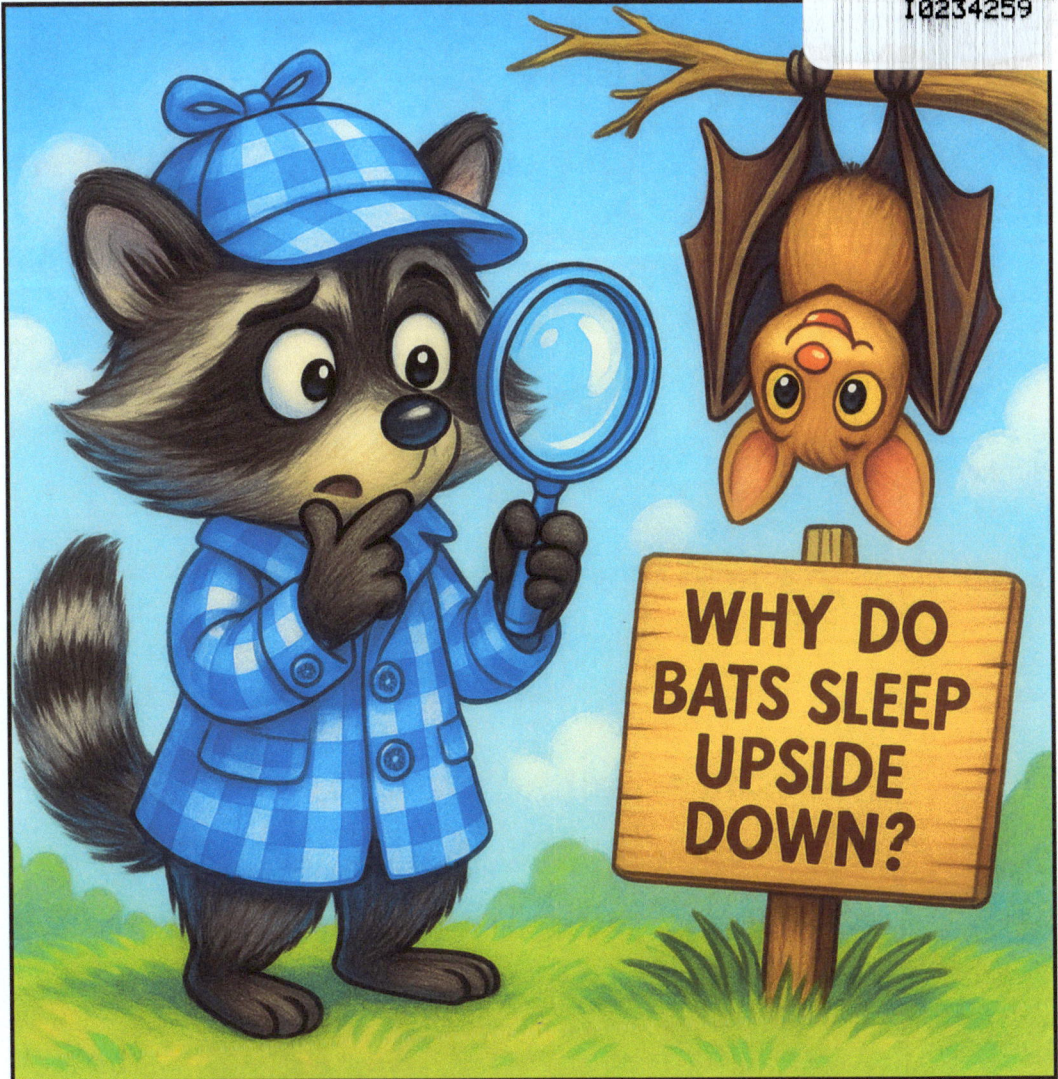

Jeannie Woodland

Author & Illustrator

When I was small and tucked in tight,
I'd dream up stories late at night.
Out from my mind, ideas would leap,
While grown-ups thought I was asleep!

I'd draw a lamp, just like you see.
Then played with ideas secretly.
An elf, a critter, a crazy clue?
A story created just for **YOU!**

Inside your mind, a lamp shines bright.
Just let your imagination take flight!
Each critter offers you a clue,
To test that zany brain in you.

How to Play the Crazy Clues Game

Guess, Giggle & Grin—You're here to WIN!

Look & Guess!
Each right-hand page shows a fun animal picture with three choices.

Take the Challenge!
Guess which choice is correct.

Turn the Page!
Check the left-hand page for the answer.

Add STARS toward winning PRIZES.
If you guess right, use star stickers or draw a star next to the correct answer.

If you have the incorrect answer, you can still win!
After you have finished the book, you can come back to the missed answers & guess again.

Crazy Clues Game
Instructions Continued

Play As Many Times As You Wish
Do this as many times as you wish till you get all of the answers correct. Remember to enter your stars when you guess it right.

Reach Your Goal!
When you reach the number of stars you need, pick a prize from the list on the next page. Your parent/s or guardian can create their list of prizes for you to pick from.

See list of prizes like puzzles & games on the next page.

Play More Games!
Find more books by Jeannie Woodland on Amazon for even more fun, games & challenges!

Play with Friends!
Get matching books & have a friendly competition to see who earns the most stars!

Attention Parents/Guardians

Make learning fun & rewarding! Set up the game:
Pick rewards from the list below or create your own.
Parents/guardians assign a star value to each prize.
Have your child pick their fun prizes before playing.
Encourage them to log stars as they progress.
When they reach their goal, they claim a prize!
They can play lots of times, alone or with friends.

1⭐ Stickers of stars, animals, or characters
1⭐ Finger puppets
1⭐ Temporary tattoos
2⭐ Glow-in-the-dark stars or glow sticks
2⭐ Origami paper with instructions
2⭐ Bookmarks with fun designs
3⭐ Crayons or colored pencils
3⭐ Bubble-making kit
3⭐ Playdough or modeling clay
3⭐ A favorite snack
3⭐ Notepads with cute designs
3⭐ Your favorite bedtime story
4⭐ Friendship bracelets
5⭐ Small toys, board games & puzzles
5⭐ A craft kit or do-it-yourself project

Why do cats purr?

Because their motors are running like racecars!
Because they are comfy, cozy, and content.
To trick you into giving them treats.

Cats purr when they are comfy, cozy and content.

purr

Warm and snug, not a care in sight,
A kitten purrs with pure delight!

Why do dogs wear collars?

To remind them of their name in case they forget.
So their best friend can find them if they get lost.
So their humans don't wander off and get lost!

To keep dogs safe and help their best friend find them if they get lost.

A stranger read his tag, and knew
This dog had love to return to.

Why do dolphins breach
out of the water?

They want to make a big splash and get you wet.
It helps them breathe & see better above water.
They like to show off their smooth moves.

Because it helps them breathe and see better above the water.

Up they go with a graceful leap,
To take a breath, and have a peek!

Why do guinea pigs jump straight up in the air?

It's how they show they are happy.
They're showing off their cool dance moves.
They have springs in their feet!

It's how they show they're happy!

When guinea pigs jump like popcorn — high.
It means they're happy. Don't ask why!

Why do horses sleep while standing?

Because they're too lazy to lie down.
So they can run away from nightmares faster!
Because their legs lock in place,
letting them rest without falling over.

Because their legs lock in place, letting them rest without falling over.

Horses' legs lock — they will not flop.
It's like they've got a built-in prop!

Why do parrots copy human's words?

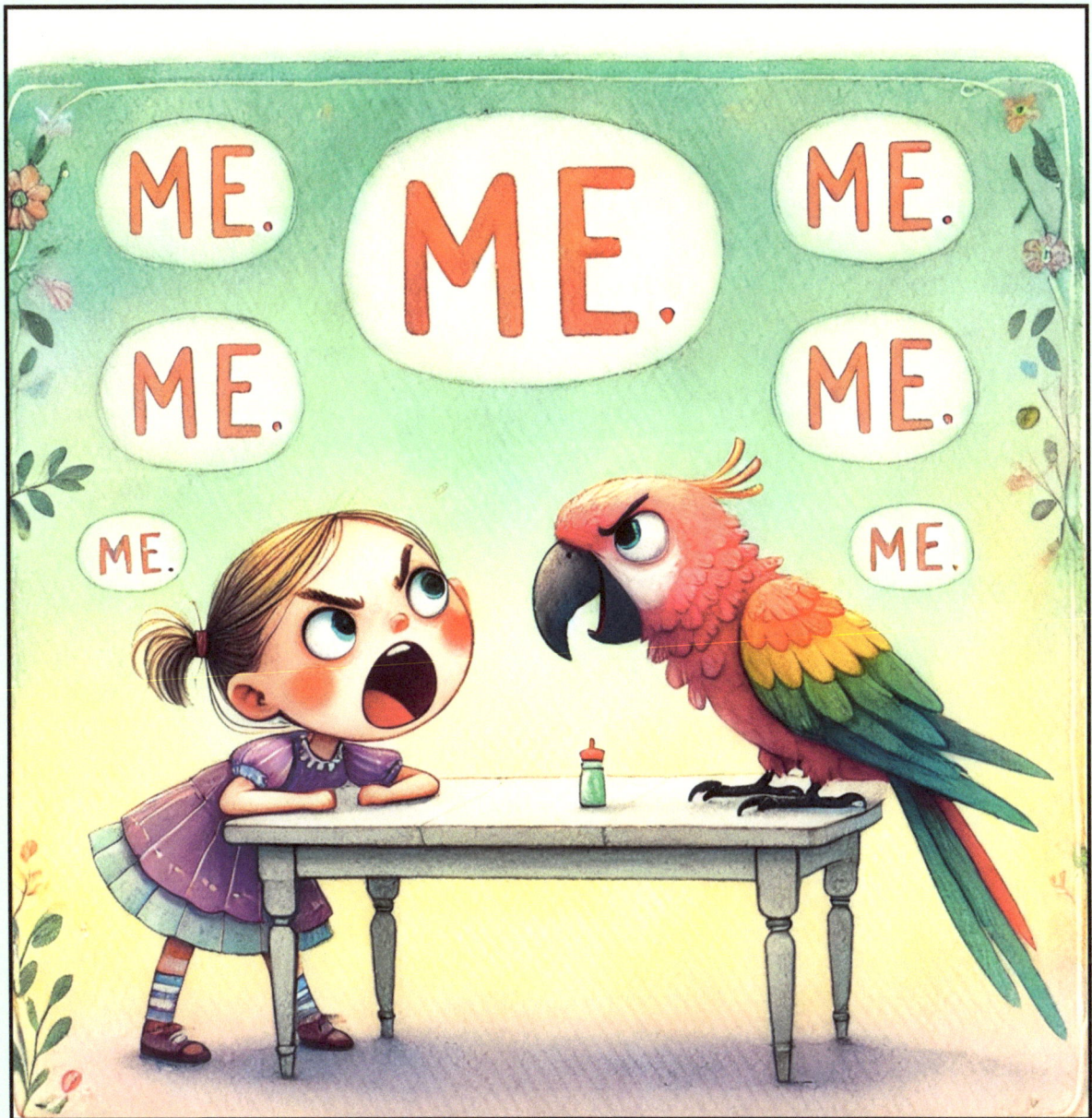

They have a special voice box that can copy sounds.
They're copycats... oops! I mean copy birds!
Because parrots are chatterboxes!

Because they have a special voice box that can copy sounds.

A puzzled pup and a bird so sly,
Both shouting "Woof!"
Now, who's the wise guy?

Why do rabbits nibble all the time?

Because they are always hungry.
Because they don't want to go to the dentist!
Because their teeth never stop growing, so nibbling keeps them short and healthy.

Their teeth never stop growing, and nibbling keeps them short an healthy.

I nibble all day, munch and gnaw,
Or else my teeth will hit the floor!

Why do sheep and lambs have fleece (that is, wool coats)?

So humans can use the wool to make fur coats.
Because natural fleece is their snuggly fur coat.
It's the perfect place for hiding fleas!

Because natural fleece is their snuggly fur coat.

No coats, no hats, no boots for snow.
Their fleece just grows from head to toe!

Why do some squirrels
have white fur?

Because they want to stand out in a crowd!
Scary animals can't spot them in the snow!
Some gene elves can only make white fur—
because they have run out of other colors!

Some gene elves can only make
white fur—they have run out of
all the other colors!

"Can you make my fur with a splash of hue?"
Gene said, "Sorry squirt, plain white will do."

How do sugar gliders glide through the air?

They jump and hope they don't crash!
They have skin stretched between their
front and back legs that help them glide.
They flap their wings like birds.

Sugar gliders have skin stretched
between their front and back legs
that help them glide through the air.

No capes, no wings, no airplane ride,
Just stretchy skin — they glide with pride!

Jeannie Woodland's Other Books

You can find more of Jeannie's books on Amazon.

Just enter 'Jeannie Woodland books.'

Here is a list of her books, plus a preview of a fun cover on the next page.

Funky Junkyard Blues
Explore Eco Fun with
Quirky Critters in Hilarious Rhyme

Momo's Wild! Wacky! Jungle Adventure
Whoooo's Haunting Hunter

Momo's Wild! Wacky! Bedtime Stories
Trouble Bubbles–Boils & Doubles

Funky Junkyard Blues
Jeannie Woodland

Eco Book

MY STORY - FOR ADULTS

Jeannie Woodland is the pen name for Kashmyra Asnani, a lifelong educator, natural wellness counselor, and fitness coach. Drawing from her experience, she began crafting whimsical, eco-conscious stories that help children discover while laughing. Her stories, quizzes, and creative activities are brimming with zany animals and irreverent humor. She ignites discovery, learning, creativity, and eco-awareness while inspiring readers to care for Mother Earth and all its wondrous creatures.

FROM GRIT TO GREEN
Kashmyra's Intriguing Eco Story

Kashmyra became an educational and eco-ed author quite by accident! Her arduous journey began when she was mysteriously immobilized with no hope. Her health challenges were rooted in an environmentally triggered illness. To distract herself from the unendurable pain, she began inventing whimsical stories in her mind, filled with quirky critters, comic scenarios, and clever twists.

Through deep research and pure grit, she began to heal. Using a pencil, she managed to write those stories down on paper. Later, she transferred them using a typewriter, and eventually onto a computer. Now she writes educational, mystery, adventure, and eco stories to ignite children's love for learning, animals, and nature.

Billions of people are impacted by environmental pollution. According to scientific research, if we don't act swiftly with awareness and care, the next generation will inherit a planet that is no longer livable; **in just 25 years!**

Publisher

Jeannie Woodland Creations

Illustrations

Illustrations by Jeannie Woodland, blending creativity with technology.

Dedication & Acknowledgments:

To my **beloved daughter, Kashmira Asnani,** whose deep commitment to the environment continues to inspire me. To Vivek, Barbara, Zayn, and the generations that follow – may your lives help shape a kinder, wiser world. To all the children across the globe: this book is for you. With special thanks to Jon Hagen, for your kindness and gentle encouragement along the way. **And in loving memory of Carlos – my dearest friend, whose love, humor, and support literally saved my life.**

ISBN 978-1-968539-07-8

Printed and Published in the USA.

www.ingramcontent.com/pod-product-compliance
Lightning Source LLC
LaVergne TN
LVHW072100070426
835508LV00002B/188